DEXTER GORDON

Jazz Saxophone Solos

Transcriptions from the Original Recording

Transcribed by Lennie Niehaus

Compilation by Eckart Rahn
Edited by Ronny S. Schiff

CONTENTS

NOTE:
Chords in parenthesis are in **concert** key for
accompaniment by "C" instruments.

ISBN 978-0-7935-5054-8

DEX MUSIC
Worldwide administration rights controlled
by Mayflower Music

HAL•LEONARD®
CORPORATION

7777 W. BLUEMOUND RD. P.O. BOX 13819 MILWAUKEE, WI 53213

Whenever and wherever Dexter Gordon appears it is an event, a celebration of life by the music that courses through his tenor saxophone which sometimes looks (but never sounds) like a toy in the hands of the handsome, 6'5" man whose frame is symbolic of his stature as an artist.

Acknowledged as the musician who, in the 1940's, synthesized the influence of Lester Young, the Coleman Hawkins School (via Herschel Evans) and Charlie Parker in translating Parker's message from the alto sax to the tenor, Dexter became the idol of a host of tenor players. Allen Eager's first Savoy recordings showed a Gordonian stamp and even Stan Getz was persuaded for a while. In Philadelphia it seemed as if Gordon was *the* model as witness Bill Barron, Jimmy Heath and John Coltrane. In New York Jackie McLean, although an altoist, was taken with Dex before even hearing Parker. And another Manhattanite, Sonny Rollins, learned important early lessons listening to Gordon.

Through tenor titans such as Coltrane and Rollins, Gordon exerted an indirect influence on the music of the next generation. In the mid-1950's, after having gone unrecorded for several years, Gordon taped some sessions that revealed he had been listening to Rollins; in 1960 an album entitled *The Resurgence of Dexter Gordon* showed an awareness of Coltrane. I later remarked that it was like receiving interest on something he had banked a long time before. In neither case had he changed his basic approach but he had kept his ears open. In 1961, when he began a series of classic recordings for the Blue Note label, he reiterated his mastery with that combination of awareness and strong allegiance to his personal muse.

To be sure there is tender strength, sophisticated subtlety, puckish punning and tidal drive blended with the engaging, disarming off-horn personality that gives Dex the marvelous capability of making people feel good. He was born Dexter Keith Gordon in Los Angeles, California on February 27, 1923. His father was a doctor who counted Duke Ellington and Lionel Hampton among his patients. Young Dexter took up the clarinet at age 13, along with the study of harmony and theory under the much respected teacher, Lloyd Reese. At 15 he switched to alto sax and two years later, in 1940, he made the move to tenor, left school and began gigging around with a local band called the Harlem Collegians. In December he was asked to join Lionel Hampton's orchestra and went on the road with the vibist, visiting New York with him in 1941 where he heard Charlie Parker in the Jay McShann band.

After leaving Hampton in 1943, Gordon returned to Los Angeles where he worked with Lee Young (Lester's drumming brother) and Jesse Price. Then, in 1944, he was a member of Louis Armstrong's big band for six months. It wasn't, however, until he joined the fabled Billy Eckstine band later in the year that he began to become a factor with both the jazz public and his fellow musicians. During his 18 months with the pioneering powerhouse of bop, sitting alongside

(at various times) Gene Ammons, Sonny Stitt, Leo Parker, Dizzy Gillespie and Fats Navarro, he was featured prominently on record in *Blowin' The Blues Away* (a tenor duel with Ammons) and *Lonesome Lover Blues*.

In 1945 Gordon located in New York and became a fixture along 52nd Street whose numerous clubs were alive with the music of Charlie "Yardbird" Parker and Gillespie. He played there with "Bird" and with his own combos, recorded separately with Diz and Bird as well as cutting a series of 78s for Savoy as a leader. In the summer of 1946 he returned to California and before he came back to New York in late 1947 he played two months in Honolulu with Cee Pee Johnson. *The Chase*, a Los Angles tenor battle with Wardell Gray made a lively dent in the jazz record market. After working and recording with Tadd Dameron's band in New York he once again went home to California in 1949 where he and Gray often teamed for club and concert jam session-type performances.

The 1950's were not an easy time for Gordon as first he wrestled with personal demons and secondly was confronted by the advent of "cool" jazz--then in vogue in L.A.--which left his gutsy, hard-driving brand of playing in short demand. By 1960, however, he began to gather momentum again, surfacing in the West Coast company of Jack Gelber's *The Connection* as composer, small group leader and actor. Cannonball Adderley produced the *Resurgence* Lp and after his first Blue Note albums, he move to New York in 1962, playing there and also using it as a base of operations for club appearances in the East.

In September of that year he journeyed to London to play at Ronnie Scott's club and continued with engagements on the Continent. Eventually he found a home in Copenhagen where he became the chief attraction at the Club Montmartre. He received great respect and appreciation in the European milieu and made periodic trips back to the United States for club work and recording which helped maintain his international reputation. But it soon became apparent that his arena was Europe. He played at the major capitals and such festivals as Berlin, Molde, Malmo, Ossiach, San Remo, Lugano, Montreux, etc. He appeared at the Newport Jazz Festival in 1970; Tangier Jazz Festival, 1972; Newport-New York, 1973; and toured Japan in 1975.

As a teacher Gordon was active with the Worker's Cultural Foundation in Malmo, Sweden and with the Jazz & Youth Society, Vallekilde, Denmark.

He repeated his roles in *The Connection* in Denmark and also made a Danish film. His television and radio appearances in Europe are too numerous to list. In the U.S. he did a *Just Jazz* segment for PBS in 1971.

Although he had played in Chicago in 1974 and Los Angeles the following year, Gordon's 1976 trip to New York was his first in four years. The media coverage accorded

D E X T E R
G O R D O N

him was more like an American jazzman visiting Europe or Japan for the first time: articles in the New York *Times;* New York *Post*; *Village Voice*; and television interviews.

He lectured at the University of Hartford and young musicians were magnetized by him wherever he played. In New York the list of his peers who came to hear him read like a Who's Who: Stanley Turrentine, Sadik Hakim, Joe Farrell, Charles Mingus, Tootie Heath, Jimmy Heath, Yusef Lateef, Cecil Taylor, Jimmy Owens, Dizzy Reece, Billy Higgins, John McLaughlin, Horace Silver, Sonny Stitt, Zoot Sims, Al Cohn, Tony Williams, Phoebe Snow, Maurice and Verdine White (of Earth, Wind & Fire) and an assortment of rock stars, to name a few.

Also in attendance was Columbia's president Bruce Lundvall, who was there as a fan as well as an involved executive. So, every night was special, particularly the three on which *Homecoming* was taped with ample support from trumpeter Woody Shaw, pianist Ronnie Mathews, bassist Stafford James and drummer Louis Hayes.

"There was so much love and elation," said Dexter. "Sometimes it was a little eerie at the Vanguard. After the last set they'd turn on the lights and nobody would move."

The excitement, reverence and warm love feeling engendered by his performances at the Village Vanguard are captured in *Homecoming*. The release of this double album was greeted with open ears by the buying public. In this age of electronics, the presence of an acoustic album on "the charts" is phenomenal, but so is Dexter Gordon.

When Dexter returned to the U.S. in the spring of 1977 he was again met by adoring fans wherever he played. He was heard on the soprano as well as the tenor saxophone. Joy continued unabated and a new recording, considered a must, was discussed. This time it would be a special studio project. It began as a septet with trumpeter Wood Shaw, a member of Gordon's American quintet and trombonist Slide Hampton, a frequent European associate, as the chief arranger. The band became an 11-piecer through a natural evolution of ideas involving many players who had worked with Dexter at one time or another: trumpeter Benny Bailey, American expatriate, imported from Europe; and vibist Bobby Hutcherson, flown in from San Francisco.

In addition, at opposite ends of the sound spectrum, came flutist Frank Wess and tubaist Howard Johnson. Hampton's arranging skill, able to spread out across such an ensemble, creates a marvelous atmosphere for Gordon and the other soloists. As producer Michael Cuscuna put it: "Dexter is one of those great blowers who is not inhibited by an expanded setting."

The result was *Sophisticated Giant*, an album everyone called "a classic." Even Dexter!

Between the time of the recording and its release Gordon won the *down beat* International Critics Poll for the first time since 1971. He was also honored by the Jazzmobile in a special concert at Grant's Tomb in New York. Then he was off to Montreux to take part in that Swiss city's pretigious jazz festival with a host of other Columbia and Epic stars including Stan Getz, Woody Shaw, Maynard Ferguson, Bob James and George Duke. All of this can be heard in *Montreux Summit*. He is featured with Shaw, Duke and Slide Hampton in his own "Fried Bananas" and with the rest of the stars in "Andromeda," Benny Golson's "Blues March" and the title track.

In 1978 Dexter was voted #1 Jazz Musician of the Year, the most prestigious indivudual *down beat* Reader's Poll Award, and for the third year in a row, was #1 winner in the tenor saxophone category. He narrowly missed winning the coveted '78 Hall of Fame category and had two albums, *Homecoming* and *Sophisticated Giant* place respectably in the Album of the Year category. Earlier in the year, Dexter was among the honorees at the White House Jazz Festival, hosted by President Carter.

Manhattan Symphonie was on the jazz charts "forever". Dexter Gordon, the romantic, had returned to New York and paid tribute with a release of well-mellowed horn combined with the fresh elements in harmony, rhythm and tonality. He hasn't just "kept up" but expanded and deepened as Dexter Gordon.

Grace and power, wit and emotion, harmonic acuity and melodic sweep: Dexter Gordon is truly a *Sophisticated Giant*.

FRIED BANANAS

from the Prestige LP7680 "MORE POWER"

Music by
DEXTER GORDON

THE APARTMENT

from the Inner City LP2025 "THE APARTMENT"

Music by
DEXTER GORDON

Moderately Bright

9

BACKSTAIRS

from the CBS LP88232 "HOMECOMING"

Music by
DEXTER GORDON

APPLE JUMP

from the Inner City LP2080 "BITING THE APPLE"

Music by
DEXTER GORDON

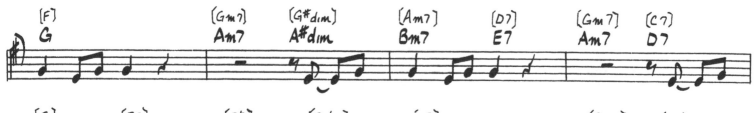

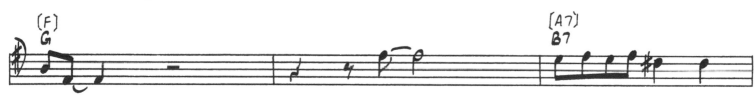

14

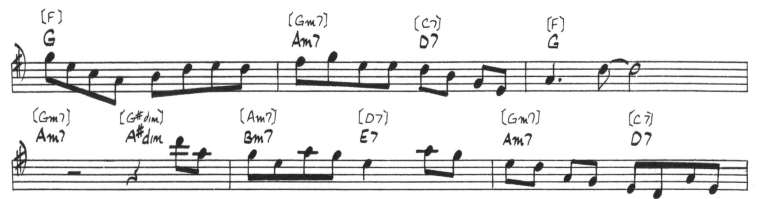

BENJI'S BOUNCE

from the Inner City LP2060 "BOUNCIN' WITH DEX"

Music by
DEXTER GORDON

16

THE CHASE

from the Prestige LP10010 "THE CHASE"

Music by
DEXTER GORDON

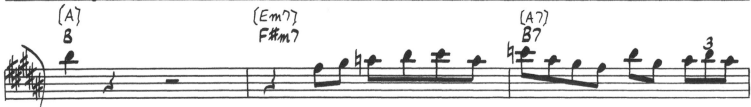

CHEESECAKE

from the Blue Note LP84112 "GO"

Music by
DEXTER GORDON

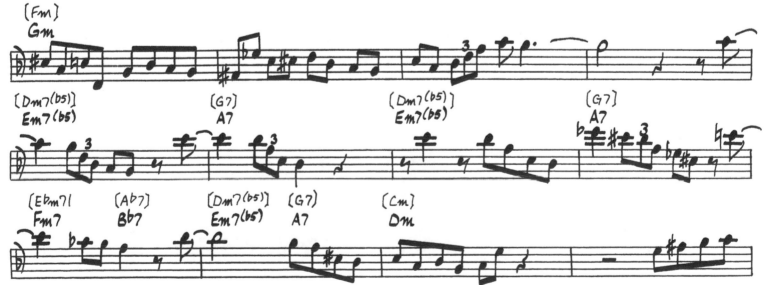

22

BOSTON BERNIE

from the Prestige LP7680 "MORE POWER"

Music by
DEXTER GORDON

FENJA

from the CBS LP88232 "HOMECOMING"

Music by
DEXTER GORDON

29

DADDY PLAYS THE HORN

from the Bethlehem LP6008 "THE BETHLEHEM YEARS"

Music by
DEXTER GORDON

Moderate Blues Tempo

DEXTER DIGS IN

from the Savoy/Arista LP2211 "LONG TALL DEXTER/THE SAVOY SESSIONS"

(2nd Version)

Music by
DEXTER GORDON

Moderate Tempo

33

THE GIRL WITH THE PURPLE EYES

from the Inner City LP2030 "MORE THAN YOU KNOW"

Music by
DEXTER GORDON

Moderate Tempo

36

LTD

from the CBS LP35608 "MANHATTAN SYMPHONIE"

Music by
DEXTER GORDON

Moderate Blues Tempo

FOR REGULARS ONLY

from the Blue Note LP84077 "DOIN' ALLRIGHT"

Music by
DEXTER GORDON

Moderate Tempo

MONTMARTRE

from the Prestige LP7623 "THE TOWER OF POWER"

Music by
DEXTER GORDON

MISCHIEVIOUS LADY

from the Spotline LP130 "THE CHASE"

Music by
DEXTER GORDON

Moderate Swing Tempo

THE RAINBOW PEOPLE

from the Prestige LP7623 "THE TOWER OF POWER"

Music by
DEXTER GORDON

Unhurried

49

SOY CALIFA

from the Blue Note LP84133 "A SWINGIN' AFFAIR"

Music by
DEXTER GORDON

WITH MOVEMENT

52

53

SETTING THE PACE

from the Savoy/Arista LP2211 "LONG TALL DEXTER/THE SAVOY SESSIONS"

Music by
DEXTER GORDON

Moderately Bright

STICKY WICKET

from the Prestige LP7680 "MORE POWER"

Music by
DEXTER GORDON

Moderate Blues Tempo

STANLEY THE STEAMER

from the Prestige LP7623 "THE TOWER OF POWER"

Music by
DEXTER GORDON

Moderate Blues

60

VALSE ROBIN

from the Prestige LP10030 "THE PANTHER"

Music by
DEXTER GORDON

Moderate Jazz Waltz

64